K Is for Kissing a Cool Kangaroo

For Mary – G.A.

For Pam and John Hodgson, salt of the earth – G.P-R.

ISBN 0-439-64021-0

12 11   6 7 8 9/0

Printed in the U.S.A.   40

First Scholastic paperback printing, March 2004

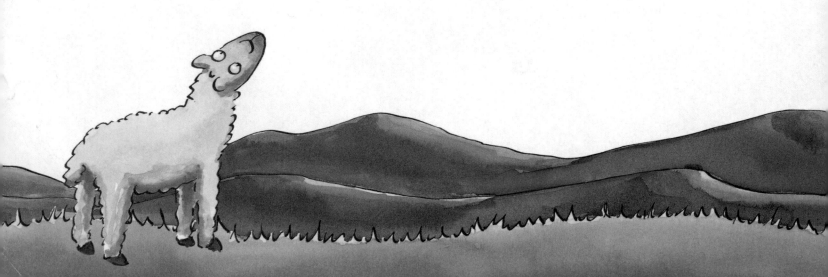

K Is for Kissing a Cool Kangaroo

By Giles Andreae   Illustrated by Guy Parker-Rees

SCHOLASTIC INC.
New York Toronto · London Auckland Sydney
Mexico City New Delhi Hong Kong Buenos Aires

Aa

a is for **apple** that grows on the tree

b is for **busy** and **big** bumblebee

Bb

d is for **dragonfly**, **daisy**, and **dream**

e is for **elephant**, mighty and strong

f is for **footprints**, one hundred **feet** long

Gg

g is for **giant**, whose **garden grows** wild

H h

h is for **holding** the **hand** of a child

Ii

i is for **igloo**, a house made of **ice**

j is for **jellybeans** – ooh, they're so nice!

Kk

k is for **kissing** a cool **kangaroo**

l is for **loving**, like Daddy **loves** you

Mm

m is for **mischievous monkey** and **mat**

o is for **octopus**, arms everywhere

P p

P is for **peaceful** and **piglet** and **pear**

q is for "Quickly, I've cuddled the Queen!"

r is for **robot** and **racing** machine

s is for **snowman** and **sister** and **snake**

t is for **teatime**, so let's have some cake!

Uu

u is for **unicorn**, **uncle**, and **udder**

V is for **vampire** whose teeth make you shudder

W whispers and waves you good-bye

Yy

y is for yeti and yo-yo and yes

and **z** is for **zebra** - now how did you guess?!

On every page there are lots of other things you may have missed.

See if you can find them . . . then check them on this list!

Aa

armadillo

antelope

ant

Cc

cake

caterpillar

clouds

bull

beetle

Bb

balloon

dalmatian

dog

Dd

duck

Ee

emerald

emu

eagle

frog

ferret

Ff

flamingo

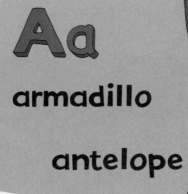

Gg

gnu

goat

giraffe

house

hamster

Hh

hyena

Ii

icicle

iguana

ibis

jester

Jj

jaguar

jam

Kk

koala

kitten

kiwi

llama

Ll

ladybug

lynx

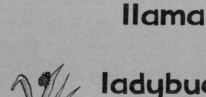

Mm

milk

mole

mango

nectarine

Nn

newt

nest

pelican

Pp

Oo

olives

owl

otter

porcupine

pirate ship

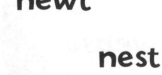

Qq

quiche

quail

quack

raccoon

rose

Rr

rat

Ss

skunk

seal

salamander

toucan

Tt

teddy bear

turtle

Uu

umbrella

vulture

violet

Vv

vole

Ww

weasel

woodpecker

wombat

X ray

Xx

Yy

yak

zinnia

Zz